Polar
Animals

By Ruth Owen

WINDMILL
BOOKS ™

New York

Published in 2015 by Windmill Books, An Imprint of Rosen Publishing
29 East 21st Street, New York, NY 10010

First Edition

Produced for Rosen by Ruby Tuesday Books Ltd
Editor for Ruby Tuesday Books Ltd: Mark J. Sachner
Designer: Emma Randall

Photo Credits:
Cover, 1, 3, 5, 6–7, 8–9, 10–11, 12–13, 14–15, 16–17, 18–19, 20–21, 22–23, 24–25, 26–27, 28–29, 31 © Ruby Tuesday Books; cover, 4–5, 6, 10, 14, 18, 22, 26 © Shutterstock.

Library of Congress Cataloging-in-Publication Data

Owen, Ruth, 1967– author.
 Polar animals / by Ruth Owen. — First Edition.
     pages cm. — (Origami safari)
 Includes index.
 ISBN 978-1-4777-9245-2 (library binding) —
 ISBN 978-1-4777-9246-9 (pbk.) — ISBN 978-1-4777-9247-6 (6-pack)
 1. Origami—Juvenile literature. 2. Polar animals in art—Juvenile literature. 3. Animals in art—Juvenile literature. I. Title.
 TT872.5.O939 2015
 736.982—dc23

                              2014014031

Manufactured in the United States of America

CPSIA Compliance Information: Batch #WS14WM: For Further Information contact Rosen Publishing, New York, New York at 1-866-478-0556

Contents

Polar Origami

Earth's two **polar regions** are possibly the most extreme **habitats** on Earth.

Antarctica, in the south, is the coldest, windiest, emptiest place in the world. The whole **continent** is covered with a thick sheet of ice. There are no trees or other plants. The Arctic area includes the northernmost parts of North America, Europe, and Russia. Here there is cold, often snowy land, an icy sea, and a massive, floating island of ice.

Surviving life in Earth's polar regions is tough, but many animals make their homes in this **environment**. In this book you can read about six animals that live at the poles. You will also get the chance to make an **origami** model of each animal.

Adult emperor penguins and chicks in Antarctica

Origami Polar Bear

Polar bears live in the Arctic. Here, there is a huge floating island of ice called the polar ice cap. The Ocean around the ice cap freezes, too, and in winter the ice spreads to join up with the land.

Polar bears hunt for seals on the frozen Arctic Ocean. They wait for seals to pop up through holes in the ice to get air. Then they attack. Polar bears are the world's largest land **predator**.

In winter, a pregnant female polar bear digs a den under the snow. Inside her den, she gives birth to one, two, or three cubs. In March or April, the family leaves the den, and the cubs come outside for the first time.

Step 1:

Fold the paper in half, crease, and then unfold. Fold the paper in half in the opposite direction, crease, and then unfold.

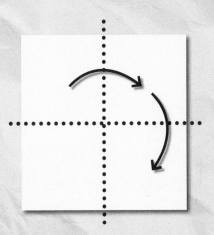

Step 2:

Fold the paper in half diagonally, and crease.

Step 3:

Fold the right-hand edge of the model back along the dotted line, and crease well.

Step 4:

Now open out the fold you've just made.

Step 5:

Next, gently squash down and flatten the open section of the model to form the polar bear's head and legs.

Gently squash down and flatten here

Head

Front legs

Step 6:

To shape the polar bear's backside, fold in the left-hand point of the model along the dotted line.

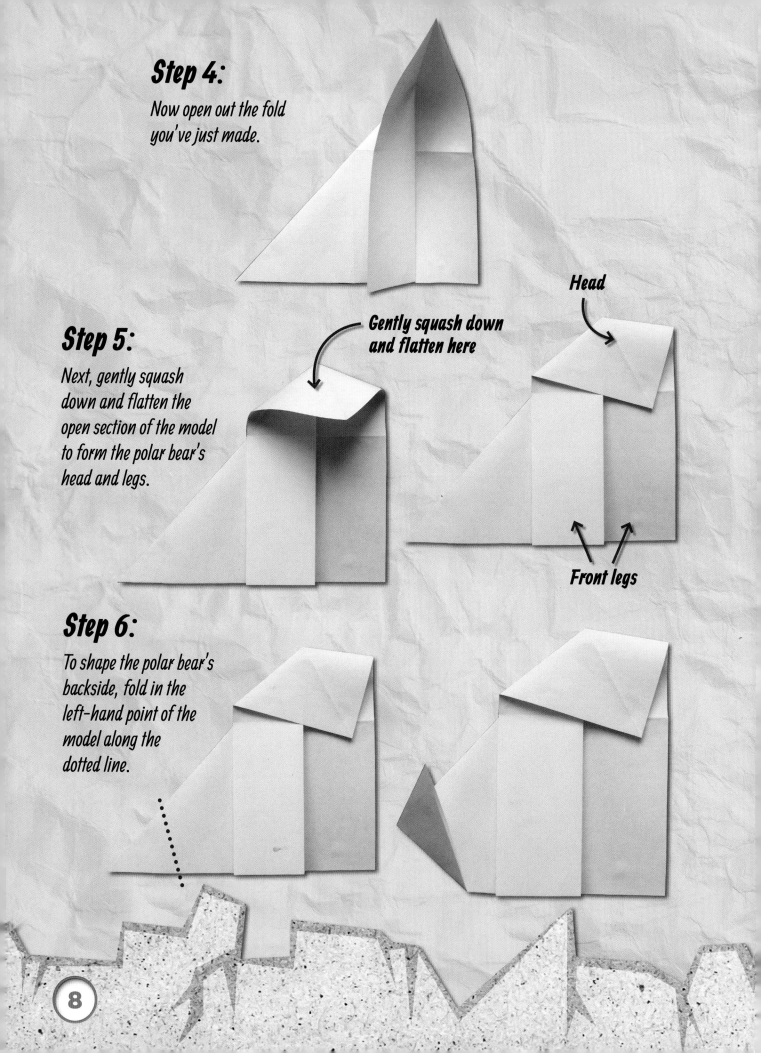

Then unfold and open out your model. Using the creases you've just made, reverse fold the point so that it is inside the model.

Then close up your model again.

Model opened out

Left-hand point of model

Step 7:

To complete your polar bear model, use a marker to draw on ears, a face, and claws. You can trim the bottom corners of the legs, too, to create paws.

Your origami polar bear is finished!

Trim the paws here

Origami Reindeer

Reindeer are a **species** of deer that live in the Arctic region. They are also known as caribou. They live in herds and are the only type of deer in which both males and females have antlers.

Large numbers of reindeer live on the Arctic **tundra**. Here, the land is covered with snow for much of the year. No trees or large plants with deep roots are able to grow. That's because just 3 feet (1 m) beneath the surface, the ground is permanently frozen. Only **lichen** and tough, low-growing plants survive on the tundra.

Reindeer feed on lichen and plants. When thick snow falls, they use their large hooves to dig in the snow and find food.

YOU WILL NEED:

• To make a reindeer, a sheet of paper that's any combination of white, gray, brown, or black

• Scissors

Step 1:

Place the paper colored side down. Fold in half, and then unfold.

Fold the top and bottom points into the center crease to make a kite shape, and crease well.

Step 2:

Now fold the top and bottom points on the left-hand side into the center crease, and crease well.

Step 3:

Turn the model 90 degrees clockwise. Then fold up the bottom point of the model to meet the top point, crease, and then unfold.

Step 4:

Open out the top right-hand triangle to create a pocket. Using the creases you've previously made, gently squash and flatten the pocket to make a point.

Pocket

Then repeat on the left-hand side.

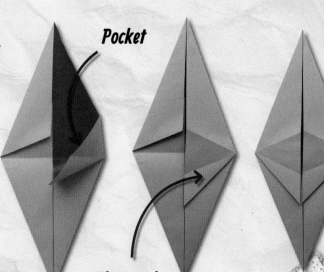

Flattened point

Step 5:

Turn the model 90 degrees clockwise, and then fold in half along the center crease.

Pointed flap

Make sure you have a flap of paper pointing toward the left-hand side of the model.

Step 6:

Neck

To make the reindeer's neck, fold up the left-hand side of the model, crease hard, and unfold.

Fold the pointed flap out of the way

Neck

Body

Now open out the model.

Using the creases you've just made, reverse fold the neck so it folds back inside the reindeer's body, and close up the model.

Step 7:

Now fold the pointed flap on the side of the model backward and down to create the reindeer's leg. Repeat on the other side.

Step 8:

To make the reindeer's head, fold down the top of the neck, crease hard, and unfold. Open out and flatten the head section. Fold the tip of the head under, then fold down each side of the head around the neck.

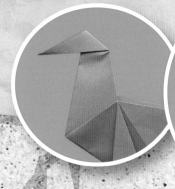

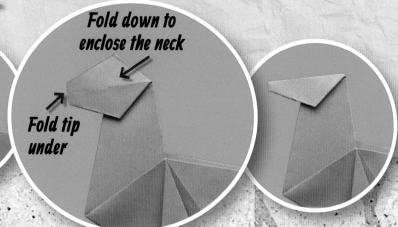

Fold down to enclose the neck

Fold tip under

To make the reindeer's antlers, cut up along the dotted line to the fold of the head. Carefully fold up the sliver of paper you've just cut. Gently separate out the layers of paper in the sliver to make the antlers.

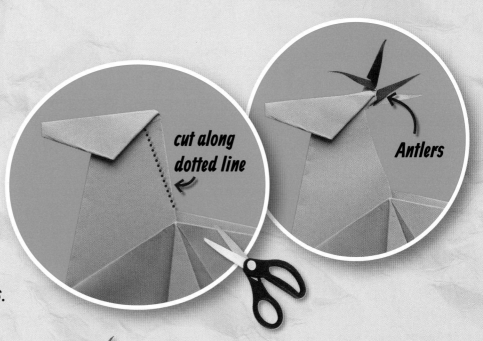

cut along dotted line

Antlers

Step 10:

Finally, make a cut up the center of the model on the right-hand side to create two points.

Fold down each point to make a leg. Then fold out the tip of each leg to make a foot.

Origami Owl

Many different species of owls live around the world. The Arctic region is home to snowy owls.

These large owls hunt for small animals, such as lemmings and mice. When hunting, snowy owls find a perch, such as on a rock. Then they use their excellent eyesight to watch for **prey**. When a prey animal comes into view, the owl takes off, flies low to the ground, and then snatches up its meal with its **talons**.

Male snowy owls have mostly white feathers. Females have white feathers with dark specks. These markings help her blend in with the snowy, rocky ground when she is sitting on her nest, which is made on the ground.

Step 1:

*Fold the paper in half,
and crease well.*

Step 2:

*Fold up side A to meet side B.
Crease well, and then unfold.*

B

A

15

Step 3:

Fold up the right-hand point of the model so that it touches the crease you made in step 2, and crease.

Step 4:

Now fold up the left-hand point of the model, and crease.

Step 5:

Fold down the top point of the model. You should only be folding down the top layer of paper. Crease well.

Step 6:

Flip the model over and turn it by 180 degrees. Fold up the bottom point, and crease.

Step 7:

Flip the model over again. Fold in the two side points of the model so that they meet in the center, and crease hard.

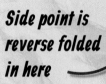

Side point is reverse folded in here

Step 8:

Now unfold the two folds you've just made and reverse fold each one so that the two points are folded inside the model.

Side point is reverse folded in here

Step 9:

Fold down the point in the center of the model to make the owl's beak. Then use the markers to draw the owl's face.

Step 10:

Finally, slide your fingers into the bottom of the model while gently squeezing the sides to open up your owl.

If you want to make a pair of snowy owls, repeat to step 10. Then draw dark speckles on your second model to turn it into a female owl.

Origami Walrus

Walruses live in freezing ocean water in the Arctic region. These huge **marine mammals** spend about two-thirds of their lives in the ocean. They spend the other third on land or on large, floating sheets of ice.

Walruses have thick pinkish-brown skin with many wrinkles and folds. A male, or bull, walrus can grow up to 12 feet (3.7 m) long and weigh 3,700 pounds (1,678 kg).

Both male and female walruses grow **tusks** made from **ivory**. An adult male's tusks may be 3 feet (90 cm) long. When a walrus wants to climb onto a chunk of floating ice, it hooks its tusks into the ice to help it haul its huge body from the water.

YOU WILL NEED:

- To make a walrus, a sheet of patterned or brown paper
- A toothpick

Step 1:

Place the paper colored (or patterned) side down. Fold in half, crease, and then unfold.

Fold the top and bottom point into the center crease, and crease well.

Step 2:

Turn the model over and fold up the bottom point to meet the top point. Crease well.

Open out here

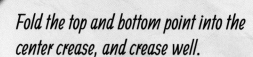

Step 3:

Turn the model over again. Open out the right-hand flap of the model. Gently squash down and flatten the flap to create a point.

Repeat on the left-hand side of the model.

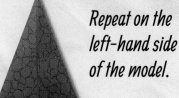

Now pick up your model, and taking hold of the back layer of paper, fold it down so that the model becomes diamond shaped.

Step 5:

Flip the model over and turn it by 90 degrees. Then fold up the bottom of the model along the center crease.

Step 6:

To make the walrus's neck, fold up the left-hand side of the model, crease hard, and unfold. Now open out the model, and using the creases you've just made, reverse fold the neck section so that it folds backward and tucks inside the body.

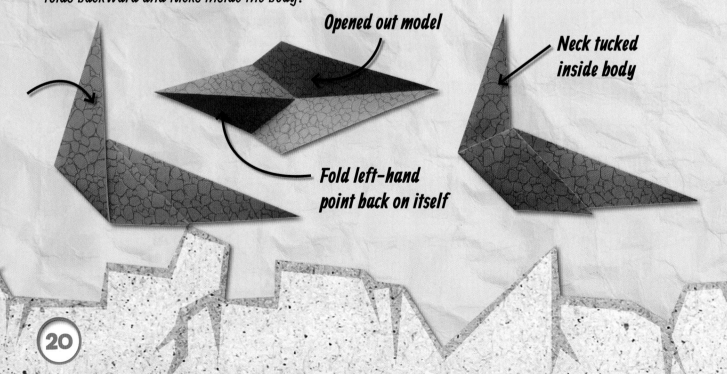

Opened out model

Neck tucked inside body

Fold left-hand point back on itself

Step 7:

To make the walrus's head, fold down the top part of the neck, crease hard, and unfold. Open out the head section, and using the creases you've just made, reverse fold the head so that it folds inward and down.

Finally, tuck in the point of the head to give the walrus a blunt nose.

Step 8:

To make the walrus's front flippers, fold the triangular flap on the side of the model toward the head. Then fold it back on itself and slightly down along the dotted line. Crease hard. Repeat on the other side.

Flipper

Tusks

Step 9:

To help your walrus stand, fold up the end of each front flipper and fold the right-hand point of the model forward

Using a toothpick, create a small hole in each side of the walrus's face. Then snap the toothpick in half and slot the two halves into the holes you're just made to become the walrus's tusks. Your origami walrus is complete.

Origami Orca

Orcas are whales that live in oceans all over the world. This includes the cold oceans around Antarctica and in the Arctic. These large marine mammals live in family groups.

An adult orca can grow to be over 20 feet (6 m) long. Adult males may have a **dorsal fin** that is taller than an adult human.

Like all mammals, orcas must breathe air. To take a breath, an orca swims to the water's surface and breathes through a **blowhole** on top of its head.

Orcas hunt for animals such as smaller whales, dolphins, sharks, seals, walruses, turtles, fish, squid, octopuses, and even sea birds.

YOU WILL NEED:

• To make an orca, a sheet of paper that's black on one side and white on the other.

Step 1:

Place the paper white side down. Fold the paper in half, crease, and then unfold.

Step 2:

Now fold in the top and bottom points of the model along the dotted lines, and crease.

Your model should look like this.

Step 3:

Fold back the points along the dotted lines, and crease.

Step 4:

Now fold down the top left-hand edge of the model along the dotted line, and crease well. Fold up the bottom left-hand edge of the model along the dotted line, and crease well.

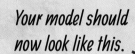

Your model should now look like this.

Step 5:

Fold the left-hand point of the model under, and crease well.

Back

Step 6:

Now fold your model in half along the center crease. Your model should look like this.

Flipper

24

Step 7:

Turn the model over so that the flippers are now at the top of the model. To make a dorsal fin for the orca, fold down the top layer of paper so that one flipper just peeks over the orca's back.

Flipper

Flipper

Dorsal fin

Flipper

Now turn the model over again, and the flipper becomes a dorsal fin.

Step 8:

Fold the top left-hand point of the orca's snout under.

Then fold the right-hand point of the model under to make a tail. Your orca is finished.

Origami Penguin

Emperor penguins live in Antarctica. These large, flightless birds spend their lives in the freezing ocean and on enormous sheets of floating ice.

Emperor penguins are the world's largest species of penguin. An adult stands about 45 inches (114 cm) tall.

These polar animals hunt in the ocean for fish, squid, and **krill**. They are strong swimmers and can dive to great depths to catch food, holding their breath for over 20 minutes.

Step 1:

Place the paper white side down. Fold in half diagonally, and crease.

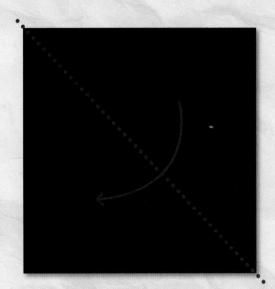

Step 2:

Fold back the right-hand point of the model so that the point meets the left-hand edge. Crease well.

Step 3:

Unfold the crease you've just made. Open out the model, and using the creases you've just made, reverse fold the right-hand point so that it folds inside the model.

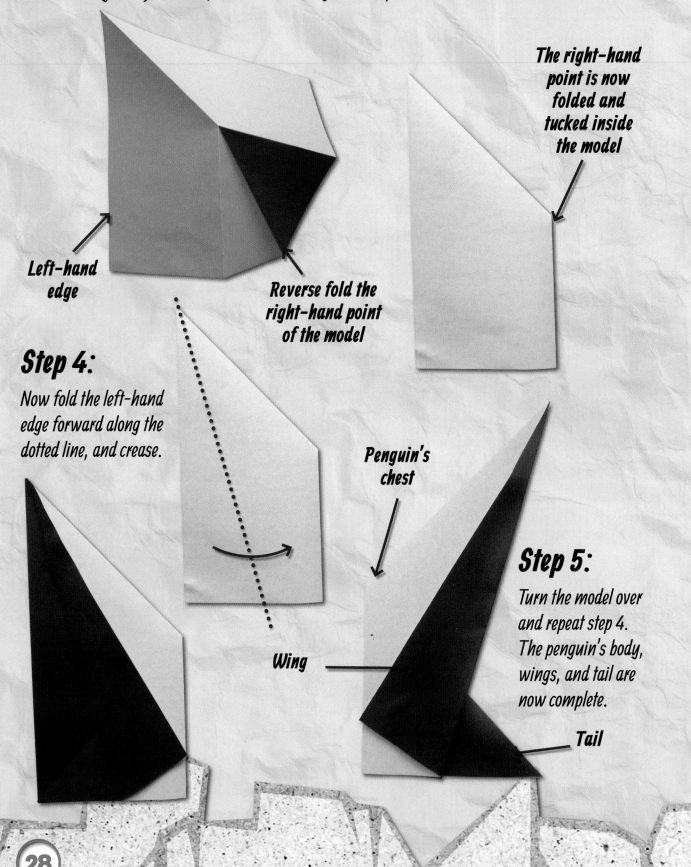

The right-hand point is now folded and tucked inside the model

Left-hand edge

Reverse fold the right-hand point of the model

Step 4:

Now fold the left-hand edge forward along the dotted line, and crease.

Penguin's chest

Step 5:

Turn the model over and repeat step 4. The penguin's body, wings, and tail are now complete.

Tail

Wing

Step 6:

To make the penguin's head, fold down the top point of the model so that the top edge of the head is parallel to the bottom edge of the model. Crease hard and then unfold.

Open out the head section of the model.

Using the creases you've just made, reverse fold the head so that it folds down over the body. The black hood of the penguin's head should now be tucked around either side of the white chest.

Step 7:

Gently open out the bottom of the model so your penguin can stand, and your model is complete.

Glossary

blowhole (BLOH-hohl)
A nostril-like hole on the head of a whale or dolphin through which the animal breathes.

continent (KON-tuh-nent)
One of Earth's seven large land masses. Africa, Antarctica, Asia, Australia, Europe, North America, and South America are all continents.

dorsal fin (DOR-sul FIN)
A triangular-shaped fin on the back of a whale or dolphin.

environment (en-VY-ern-ment)
The area where plants and animals live, along with all the things, such as weather, that affect the area.

habitats (HA-buh-tats)
The places where animals or plants normally live. A habitat may be the ocean, a jungle, or a backyard.

ivory (YV-ree)
A hard, white material. The tusks of walruses and elephants are made of ivory.

krill (KRIL)
Tiny, ocean-living, shellfish.

lichen (LY-ken)
Plant-like living things that grow on rocks and trees.

marine mammals (muh-REEN MA-mulz)
Warm-blooded animals that live in the ocean, have backbones, breathe air, and feed milk to their young.

origami (or-uh-GAH-mee)
The art of folding paper to make small models. Origami has been popular in Japan for hundreds of years. It gets its name from the Japanese words *ori*, which means "folding," and *kami*, which means "paper."

polar regions (POH-lur REE-junz)
The most northern and southern places on Earth. There are icy seas and areas of frozen land at the poles.

predator (PREH-duh-tur)
An animal that hunts and kills other animals for food.

prey (PRAY)
An animal that is hunted by another animal as food.

species (SPEE-sheez)
One type of living thing. The members of a species look alike and can produce young together.

talons (TA-lunz)
Claws on a carnivorous, hunting bird such as an owl or eagle.

tundra (TUN-druh)
A rocky, treeless, boggy landscape of low-growing plants. Below the surface is a layer of permanently frozen soil called permafrost.

tusks (TUSKS)
Long, pointed teeth that grow outside of an animal's mouth.

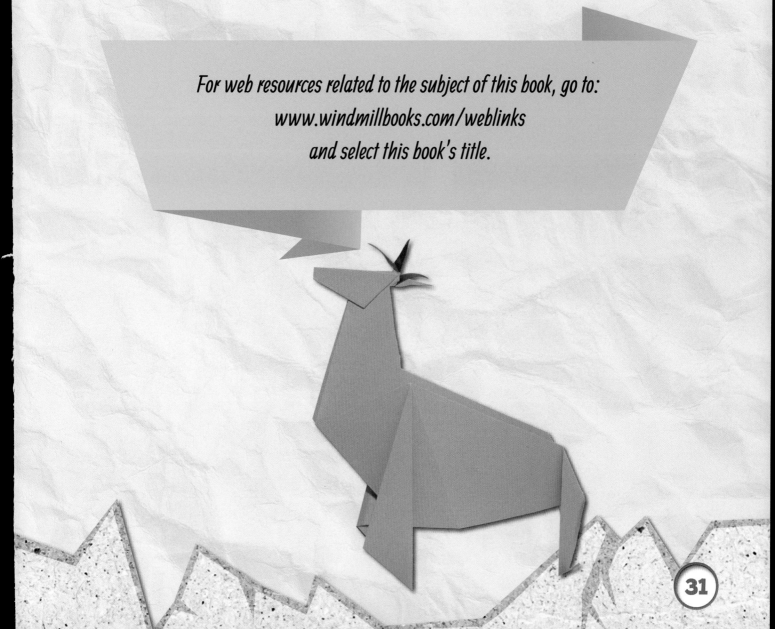

For web resources related to the subject of this book, go to:
www.windmillbooks.com/weblinks
and select this book's title.

Read More

Allgor, Marie. *Endangered Animals of Antarctica and the Arctic*. Save Earth's Animals. New York: PowerKids Press, 2013.

de Lambilly-Bresson, Elisabeth. *Animals in Polar Regions*. Animal Show and Tell. New York: Gareth Stevens Publishing, 2008.

Owen, Ruth. *Polar Bears*. Dr. Bob's Amazing World of Animals. New York: Windmill Books, 2012.

Index